2022 By Harriet Brooks
How Did The Fox Get in My House

All rights reserved . No portion of this book may re-produced , stored in a retrieve al system, or transmitted in any form or by means -electronic , mechanical ,photocopy, recording , scanning, or other -except for brief quotations in critical reviews or articles ,with out prior permission of the publisher .

Paperback
ISBN - 979-8-9852174-2-1

Library of Congress Control Number

Table of Contents

Introduction	5
Fond Memories of the Past	9
The Fox	25
The Fox of Incest	29
The Fox of Toxic Relationships	45
The Fox of Fear	55
The Fox of Counterfeit Love	59
The Fox of Dysfunction	69
The Fox of Bitterness	85
The Fox of Deep Depression	95
The Fox of Low Self Esteem	99
A Place in Your Heart	107
for Seniors	107
A Happy Place	111
About The Author	117
Resources	119

Introduction

The author is a woman who is now in her senior years but grew up in a fast pace city on the East Coast with lovely parents and siblings who looked forward to the summer visits with their grandparents. She takes you through a walk down memory lane with the memorable experiences that she and her siblings experienced. Their grandparents were farmers and very loving people who brought joy, taught them valuable lessons, and helped them experience lots of fond memories with each visit that they will never forget . In fact, they have been passed a number of those experiences on to their children and grand children as well. Watching the agriculture process of preparing the ground for planting, planting seeds, nurturing, and watching them grow from the fruits of all our labor was fascinating to each one of them.

Her mission is to create awareness, give messages, resources, and solutions to those who may be or have been victimized by a fox or foxes that have entered their homes or heart with the purpose of destroying them.

How Did The Fox Get In My House is designed and written for the readers to know that there is an escape route that will lead them to emotional health and freedom from being out of a state of entrapment, low self esteem, depression, and bitterness.

The writer exposes various situations that may have been used against her readers as a vacuum to suck out his or her life, purpose, and destiny for his or her life and gives her readers options to escape, and catapult them to emotional freedom for them to obtain their goals and aspirations.. The writer also gives resource information that is vital for the well being of each reader. She breaks down walls of fear that started in the early ages of many.

She leaves each reader with the message of getting into a happy place and staying there despite the challenges or road blocks of discouragement. Also Instructs them how to break the chains of bondage and strive toward a better life. Constantly lets them know that what ever the dream or aspiration that she seemed shattered or never would become a reality that it is not where you start but where you finish and those goals which seemed like dreams can be achieved.

She encourages the seniors who feel that they are nothing but throw aways because of their age, lets them know that they are important because they all have a lot of wisdom and knowledge to help the youth of our generation in a number of ways by showing them how to explore their gifts and talents by developing the things they like to do.

Fond Memories of the Past

Do you have any fond memories of things that not only impacted your life but followed you as you became an adult.

As the school year would end, each summer ,my siblings and I would be filled with excitement as we prepared to visit with our grandparents who owned and operated a farm. We could hardly sleep the night before leaving for the trip.

Just think, no more hustle and bustle of city living for two whole months. Escape from the noise of honking horns while sitting in traffic, the smell of diesel fuel from delivery trucks going about their daily task, and most of all a chance to get away from the stress of always rushing to get from one place to another. City life seemed to be one be rush. People seemed to have very little or no patience at all; everything seemed like it was an urgency. We would be away from nervousness, and frustration and enjoy a few months of total relaxation despite helping with all the farming chores. The atmosphere would be totally calm. What a relief; we could literally take our time without moving as though ever second counted.

There would be time to clearly progress thoughts, ideas, and dreams of what and who we would like to become as well as the path(s) to take to achieve those goals.

The farm was filled with every thing imaginable. But here is one of things that we would never forget; we would be awaken to the aroma of fresh coffee, hot homemade bread, sausage, eggs, served with the jelly that grandma would get from the storage cabinet of preserves that had been prepared after every harvest of the fruits. Fresh orange juice would be squeezed daily. Homemade biscuits dripping in butter the was churned by grandma herself.

Grandma's Sunday dinners were the best. We picked fresh vegetables from the field while our grandfather would get a chicken from the chicken coupe. The aroma of dinner cooking could be smelled for a least a mile down the road where they lived. She allowed us to choose what type of dessert we wanted after dinner and prepared what ever we selected.

Our grandmother had the personality of a warm, kind hearted, sweet person who loved to make people happy. Her radiant smile would lift anyone with a hung down head; and that what she always did.

Although she was short in stature her heart was very large. She was a blessing to all those who ever came into her presence.

She rode her her bicycle and did jazzercises until she was well in her nineties. She could go up and down the stairs at a fast pace with out getting winded. Can you imagine that ?

She never experienced any corns, bunions, callouses or any type of foot disorders from wearing shoes that were to tight to keep up with the fashions or latest styles.

It was amazing to us that her hair was still black as she aged. Then it was filled with a salt and pepper color that women pay beauty salons lots of money to attain. With all the stress that we contend with in today's society, the gray comes in at an early age. Father time seems to change our appearance drastically.

Some women don't want to ever age and they do everything to avoid getting older but grandma just praised God for her life and how He kept her in good health as she aged. A number of women fear the process of aging so they use fountain of youth creams, get face lifts , tummy tucks, breast implants, and do everything that they possibly can to slow down or stop the aging process.

I just don't why people feel that they will never grow old. She was always thankful for the smallest to the largest thing she ever attained during her life time. Grandma aged very gracefully. Her feet were perfect; with out bunions , corns, or callouses on the bottom of her feet. Her skin didn't have very many wrinkles at all. We were amazed how sharp her mind was in her nineties. She was able to write letters, send greeting cards, and communicate with us by phone.

The youth department at her church especially enjoyed the bake goods that she made for all their Easter, Thanksgiving, and Christmas programs on a wood burning stove. As time went on, our parents purchased a gas stove with a range oven but she felt comfortable using her wooden stove and asked them not to remove it. They explained that times were changing and this was for her benefit to make things easier. She finally agreed to keep it only if she could have her wood stove as well.

Neither of our grandparents had a formal education but God was with them both and blessed them tremendously. Our Grandfather owned and operated a business which had several plots of land. He would market his crops to canneries and his live stock to meat packing houses. A large portion of those proceeds were used to continually make additional purchases of land to expand the business. He hired seasonal part time workers to pick the produce from the crops and slaughter meat that he marketed every year.

The soil there from the earth was extremely rich and you could tell by the texture and taste of all the produce he grew as well as the live stock. We watched him plow up the fallow ground of the fields to prepare the land for planting his crops with a mule and only one plow before he was able to purchase a tractor and equipment that would do the work and save him from so much manual labor. He often expressed the importance of letting the land rest for seven years once a crop had been utilized ; So that the land would not be stressed out and produce a failing crop. We watched the sun peep through the dawning of day with her beautiful ray of sunshine casting her rays of light on the crops with care not letting any of them get scorched.

The rain showered down like an under ground sprinkling system. It is amazing how mother nature has nurtured everything since the beginning of time. The crops were never flooded out but took on just enough water to give them what they needed.

He claimed that land that is stressed from being over worked will not produce a good harvest. He grew corn, tomatoes, white potatoes, onions, water melons, cucumbers, peas, sweet potatoes, and cabbage just name a few.

We never knew the secret of why he never used pesticides or insecticides ever on any of the crops. We only experienced an occasional worm or two in a tomato. Amazing !!!!!! but nothing else. God blessed the labor of his hands. There were never locust or insects that destroyed any of his crops.

He and his employees started their day of work at 4:00 am in the morning and worked until 2: 00 pm in the afternoon. They used the moon as their light which shinned pretty bright in those days. They worked before the temperature got too hot. And wouldn't know it, grandma always had a wonderful lunch prepared at the end of each work day.

Sometimes the lunch looked like a Sunday dinner. Fresh vegetables, salad, fried chicken, mashed potatoes, home made iced tea, fried corn, home made biscuits, fresh fruit, and an assortment of desserts. Wow, it seemed like an all you could eat buffet dinner at the dining room table.

We were introduced to multi-tasking with out any idea what we were being prepared for. How grateful we were as we became adults and entered the work force.

You could pick a tomato out of the field and eat it right there. The crops he produced had the best taste we ever experienced.

We were eating organic food and had no Idea what we were eating. In addition to the produce, he had cows, pigs, chickens, ducks, horses, and a mule.

None of the animals were ever dirty or had any type of a bad odor. The animals had to be cared for and groomed regularly. Because the food that they ate was free from any chemicals, pesticides, or hormones ;they never had a foul order.

Because there wasn't the refrigeration that we have now, the meat was preserved with salt and placed into what was called a smoke house; none of the meat ever spoiled.

When it came time to slaughter, the employees knew how to cut each animal perfectly into the various portions without any butcher training. Could you imagine eating rib eye, and porter house steaks without chemicals, hormones or any type antibiotics in anything. The taste is totally different from those who have been injected with such chemicals.

At the close of each summer, we were sadden to have to leave each year after having such a good time with our grandparents. The days and nights were always filled with lots of fun of which there was always new things to learn about the farm. We played games and talked to our grandparents as we listened to stories about their child hood.

As we returned to the city at the end of our break, grandpa would ask our parents what type of meat we would like when they went to slaughter.

Our father would give him a list and arrange for the pick up when they were ready.

While we were there, the experience of watching a hen lay eggs was truly fascinating. There was nothing like going to the hen house to gather fresh eggs for breakfast or grandma baking needs. The hen (s) laid eggs that were had double bright yellow yokes and very large. They were corn fed, not caged but had the freedom of walking around in a specific area of the yard that was just for them.

As we assisted with various chores on the farm, grandpa always warned and encouraged us to ensure that the hen houses were locked and the doors securely fastened to keep predators away. Why was this so important to grandpa? We never really understood until later in each of our lives.

The tomatoes, cucumbers, and corn we picked made the best salads you ever ate in life; everything was just so full of life. They were just so fresh words or adjectives cannot be used to give justice to describe the flavor.

At that time the cows were milked by hand, the cream taken off for milk and grandma churned it into butter and made butter milk . Later she took the cream and made home made ice cream which we had to be churned manually by hand using rock salt and blocks of ice in an ice cream maker. What a treat; the work was well worth it because It was the best flavor ever.

While grandpa tended the crops and farm animals, grandma had a vineyard full of luscious strawberries, grapes, blueberries, and raspberries of which she canned and made all types of jellies , preserves. and an assortment of pies. I can still visualize the luscious grapes hanging from the lattice which was a sight to behold.

In addition, there was her beautiful flower garden that could have won a prize in the House Beautiful magazine. Jellies, vegetables, and fruits were stored and used during the winter months when the weather was cold and brutal. Soups , casseroles, and stews was also a part go her menu. There was also an array of delicious fruit salads they were on the menu several nights for dinner. They were large and so luscious our eyes were filled with excitement every time we saw them; but arrayed in all types different colors.

There are so many fond memories of Grandma cooking Sunday dinner after which the family would sit on her porch , enjoy the afternoon breeze, watch the wind blow through the trees as they would bow to each other giving heed to mother nature as grandpa told stories of his child hood as well as the struggles of a young boy growing up in the southern part of the south. The sky looked as though God took time to use His divine color pallet of blue and with His fingers splashing hints of fluffy white clouds that were breath taking. The air was so fresh and clean which is rare these days void of any type of smog. No one suffered from allergies or sinus conditions of any kind which was great. Major digestion or stomach problems rarely existed during those days.

Family time was a very important part of our culture. Game nights were always very interesting. We played the game of monopoly which took up the entire evening. Grandma served cookies and milk as she watched us learn the dynamics of the game.

Other nights we learned the art of playing checkers and dominos but the hardest game to play was chess.

Only a few of us mastered the game but we tried very hard.

Family time was very special and very memorable . We ate as a family all gathered around the dining room table which is rare these days. Most families eat at separate times and the children order pizza or junk food as their dinner meal and eat in their rooms in front of a computer screen. It was also a time to express ideas, thoughts of what we wanted to do as we grew into adulthood.

Just before the close of the summer with our grandparents, our grandfather took us to a bay near by that was opened to the public to those who lived in the area. He taught us how to fish, dig for clams, and oysters. The flavor of which was just as lovely as everything else we had eaten. We learned the technique of fishing and the art of patience. It is very interesting that patience is an important trait that all of us should possess and hold dear to our hearts; without patience, we can embark upon dangers that could destroy us.

During the last few days before leaving, we sat on the porch and enjoyed the cool breeze and the changing of the wind from summer to fall. We watched the birds organize their flight pattern to prepare to leave for the incoming winter months and find a new home. The leaves on the trees took on colors that spelled out autumn in all her beauty.

As our summer vacation came to a close, there weren't enough tissues to catch all the tears that flowed from each of our eyes. The time with them was so very special. The memories of our stay will never fade away. The love, care, and valuable lessons we learned will always be dear to each of our hearts. We never wanted to leave and cried as the car went out of view as we saw them wave good bye.

All of a sudden , the times seemed to change drastically It seemed that things changed over night. Companies implemented methods to manufacture everything as fast as possible to increase inventory and profit margin. They were only concerned about the bottom line; Marketing Teams were hired to perform time studies and strategize the best means of helping the companies succeed at their projected goals. Artificial and substitute products became a part of the ingredients of almost every product sold in stores and our markets. Owners became more interested in how much revenue their bank accounts increased every quarter than the true quality of their products which was a major priority.

Although we ate the foods of that day, we were not fat or over weight at all. There weren't fats and trans fats or hormones to increase the size of animals in a short time to increase sales volume; Nor were vegetables put in hot houses but grew from good old mother earth.

Now a days everyone is weight conscious and worried that he or she may not be eating healthy. Fitness centers have all kinds of advertisements to intrigue and encourage our society to become conscious of his or her weight. T V. advertisements consistently talk about heart heath, the damage of arteries , high blood pressure and obesity. Just think, it wasn't that long ago that we walked to school which was at least 3 miles each way; despite the weather conditions. On the East Coast rain or snowy weather wasn't a problem but we seemed to weather the storms unless it snowed more than 5 inches. We built snow men and always made snow ice cream because of the clean air . Now a days we are afraid to make or eat snow ice cream for fear of all the impurities that might be in it. The majority of us that lived during that era didn't have a weight problem.

We walked a lot of places whether or not we owned a car or not. We were in great physical shape; this helped in so many different ways. Our generation was in great physical shape from all the exercise we go which eliminated all sorts of physical illnesses from the lack there of; You never heard of knee or hip replacements as you do today.

However, In today's society a large percentage of people have work out equipment in their garage or a designated area in the house for working out.

Unfortunately not many people are faithful in his or her exercise program. They seem to fall off the wagon of consistency very fast. Heart attacks, strokes, and high blood pressure is the plight of almost every household.

The discussion of our summer at grandma and grandpa's home at the dinner table was a topic of discussion for weeks after we returned back home. Conversations of memories that we we will never forget went from each one of the siblings. We were always learning new things that captured the hearts of every one who heard of our adventures. We always learned so much every time we visited our grandparents during summer break.

Grandpa and Grandma were people of integrity who taught us the value and characteristics of having a good one. They were highly respected by all through out their neighbor hood and surrounding cities.

Our dad always asked whether or not we were on our best behavior and if there were any encounters with any foxes during our stay. We expressed how grandpa always encouraged us to secure the hen houses to avoid any entry of a fox or predator. He explained that it would be detrimental if any of those doors were left ajar. He explained that if a fox or predator were to have entry that his poor chickens would not stand a chance to defend themselves or lured them away.

Fortunately there weren't any encounters. Thank the Lord!!!!

We learned so much from our grandparents that we have taught our children and their children's children. Integrity and truth was part of who they were. They expressed the importance of integrity and the determination to follow our dreams and aspirations. Their legacy will live on through out all of our generations. We planned to continue to teach our children, grand children and their children. We want to carry out the legacy that they started by adhering to all values that they taught us.

The Fox

Characteristics of a Fox

Foxes are members of the Canidae family, which means they're related to wolves, jackals, and dogs. They're medium-sized, weighing anywhere between 2 and 24 pounds, with pointy faces, lithe frames, and bushy tails.

According to the University of Michigan, the red fox not only runs at 30 miles per hour but also has the ability to jump over obstacles that are two meters high. They have claws on both their front and hind feet for getting good traction in the earth. Their front feet have five claws, and their back have four.

Goggle also gives a vivid description of the fox. They are sly, cunning, and extremely manipulative. They go after their prey before dawn or dust dark; Always looking for those who make up the weakest link; they study their prey closely and look for an opportunity to attack. After attacking their prey they only leave evidence that they went in for the kill. A residue of feathers, and blood are the evidence that he struck after he attacked chickens. You just learned about the characteristics of an animal fox.

Unfortunately, there are human foxes with two legs and two feet whose motives are to deceive, manipulate, steal, kill, hurt, and even destroy their prey. They look for victims who are sad, lonely, and depressed; Which one of these foxes have you let in your heart or even your home.

In the following chapters please see how you may have fallen victim to any of these circumstances. These foxes may have moved in and taken up residence and refused to move from your house , emotions, your children and your family members.

The foxes in this book are used as a metaphor to describe what can happen if he is let into your home or heart. There is a lot of damage which plays a part in his destructive mannerism that is beyond repair. But it can all be avoided with education of his tactics and awareness of how to handle him.

Please don't let him in any of your affairs

The Fox of Incest

The ugly fox of incest entered the home of Eunice a young teen ager who had just entered high school. Eunice and her sister lived together with their mother and father which was where they both had a miserable home life.

Eunice's mother was paralyzed and bed ridden as a result of a bad car accident. Her father set up a hospital bed in their downstairs living room for easy access for the nurses who came every day to give the father assistance. Both daughters helped to make their mother as comfortable as possible in between the nurses visits and care. She and her sister hated the fact that their mother was in that condition. They couldn't help but remember when things were much different. Especially when their mother was able to move around and live a normal life.

This took a toll on both sisters. It was an emotional whirl wind that swept the two of them up emotionally. Just seeing their mother in that condition never being able to walk, stand, cook meals, unable to attend parental school functions was quite depressing. Their mom had always been the supporter of both girls; she baked brownies and cookies for the students many times when she dropped them off at school. She also volunteered at the school as a teacher's assistant the days that she was not at work.

Adjusting to this new home life was a lot to bear. Eunice had no Idea that her home life would change even more for the worst.

Home life started to change again as Eunice entered high school. It became a living night mare and a horrific experience that she wanted erased from her memory.

Her father had made strict rules enforcing them as though he were a master sergeant in the army. She was not allowed at to attend school dances , plays, activities or go to any of the football games after school. Her father insisted that she come home immediately when school was dismissed. His excuse was that her mother needed she and her sister to be there for assistance . Her father never wanted neither Eunice or her sister to live a normal life of a teenager; to date or have a boy friend. He always changed the subject and made it seem like a terrible thing for both of them to do. If they would get caught with any young man carrying their books or engaging in a conversation, he would become enraged and punish them sometimes for weeks. How much more emotional pain could he inflict on us as she pondered over the harsh treatment.

Eunice couldn't figure it out until one night while sleeping, her father came in her bed room and raped her. She was terrified, scared, bruised and ashamed. All she could think of was that he took my virginity away as she cried for hours. After the incident , She stayed in the bath tub for hours washing her body with the false sense of hope that this ugly thing that happened would go away. The smell of his body odor and sour breath stayed with her for hours. For hours she couldn't stop reliving the incident every time it happened. What did I do for this awful thing to happen to me she asked her self over and over.

Her father swore her to secrecy and threaten to kill her sister and her mother if she told any one what happened.

This damaged her from that time and through out most of her adult life. She felt dirty and ashamed. She didn't want to leave the bath tub but washed for hours and hours crying uncontrollably.

I just wanted to wash all that happened to me away she proclaimed . Tears covered her pillow that night and nights after for months. Her father kept warning her not to tell anyone of their encounters or there would be serious consequences.

He took my virginity that I dreamed of sharing with some one that I truly loved one day in a marriage relationship as the tears wet her pillow night after night.

She wasn't allowed to go any where or do anything that a normal teen ager would or could do kept being her despairing cry.

Going to school emotionally drained was her plight every day. She did everything she could to hide what was going on. Layers and layers of make up was applied daily to cover up the tear stained face and constant destress that showed up on her face every day. Little did she know that the application of all the make up that she applied would never take away the pain she felt of that horrific experience.

Emotionally distraught, Eunice didn't know what to do. Her behavior was that of a mentally sick young woman who never wanted to socialize with any one but chose to stay as far away from as many people as she could.

She stayed to her self keeping a distance from her peers feeling like a dirty rag that had been used and then thrown away. As time went on, there was no self worth or fight left in her. She didn't feel validated or love for herself.

This sick behavior from her father continued and seemed like it would ever end. Night after night her father entered her room and pleasured himself with her. As she tried to fight him off, he always over powered her. The more he molested her, the worst she felt, just sick to her stomach; she would vomit each time after the incident occurred.

He was a horrible pedophile that took advantage and control of his daughter. Sex to Eunice was thought of as an awful ugly nasty thing. Each incident didn't make it any better. Her attitude became bitter, wroth, and angry at the sight of any man she saw. Every one that she came in contact with got the message written on her face that she didn't want to be bothered and was totally uninterested.

Even though she didn't want any part of sex in her life ever ; It is very clear that God gave each human being the tools to experience a blissful sex life when the time is right. God made this an awesome expression of intimate love between a man and a woman but the encounter with her father made it seem so dirty and disrespectful that she didn't want to have any part of it.

Hatred began to arise in her heart for the man that she once loved and respected. She was so proud to have a father like him, so she thought until that awful thing happened. Why oh Why would he do this to me she asked herself?

Before this awful experience there were dreams of meeting a wonderful young man who would be a marriage partner for life. This would be a person full of love, care, and lots of compassion. He would fit the mold of priest, protector, and provider that every woman longs for. She would ultimately share in the bliss of love making with her husband.

Unfortunately she developed an attitude like most sexually abused women and began to feel like all men were like dogs without regard to the real love and care for women.

Eunice's emotions were so twisted; if a young man would speak to her or try to engage in a conversation, it caused her to go into a panic almost unable to speak. Bitter, angry, and confused it triggered a replay of the awful experience of her father molesting her over and over. The deep dark secret was a plaque that haunted her over and over and put her in a dark emotional place. Suffering in silence was the absolute worst thing that could happened aside from being used as a sex toy.

All types of thoughts filled her head of what should be done to escape this horrible abusive prison. She felt entrapped in a web struggling to get out with out a way of escape.

Our high school counselors were great. We had counselors who had the interest of the students at heart. The Idea of their successes pulled on the heart strings of each of them. They spent countless hours looking for projects and curriculum that would catapult us into career paths to prepare us for a successful adult life once we entered and left college.

My counselor encouraged me to set goals that would help me achieve an academic goal that would propel me into a career that would be quite attractive. Despite the craziness in the home, amazingly the struggle was hard but some how I managed to mustard up enough strength to get good grades making the honor role and the deans list every semester which was a miracle despite the fear and distress that loomed over me every day.

My school counselor was interested in seeing everyone succeed. There wasn't any thing that she wouldn't do to see to it that each student achieved his or her career path.

Fortunately with her help and guidance I was able to get a full scholarship that paid tuition and housing at a prestigious university for four years. My heart was filled with joy and amazement when the counselor gave me the good news.

The next three years of high school seemed like a bright light was shining at the end of the tunnel. My focus was on my grades and leaving the prison that was lodged in our home.. I chose a career that would help rescue young women who had been victimized just like me. There was a determination to stop as many pedophiles from damaging as many young girls for life as I could. I had dreams of opening up a safe haven home for girls with therapy sessions to help them through the trauma they encountered and move on into a life of happiness and freedom from the horrific life style that they had encountered.

Renderings of rooms, decor, therapy sessions, resources, and helps filled my vision board as new thoughts and ideas would some day become a reality.

God had truly blessed me. Because of the blessing that had been provided; the time seemed to go faster than I thought. As I blotted out the encounters with my father, my thoughts were filled with my escape and moving out the house of horror that caused me so much grief.

Because I concentrated on my dreams , graduation was finally here; Joy filled my heart as I left for college. Tears streamed down my face as I approached the university and my new home for the next four years. Finally I was out of the bondage of being molested by my father, suffering in silence and hiding the deep dark secret.

There was a deep desire to bring my sister to live with me the moment that I graduated , find a job, and get an apartment. She would be free of any type of physical, sexual, or emotional trauma ; It would give her a jump start in living a normal happy life.
As I pondered, thoughts of also taking care of my mother and seeing that the last years of her life was full of joy to see the accomplishments of her children and making things as comfortable as possible.

College was a stepping stone to propel me into the destiny of my dreams.

While in college the assigned room mates for each remaining semester was great. We all had some of the same things in common.

However, we never shared the misfortunate of what happened in each of our homes while growing up which I was glad.

The school set up therapy sessions for all the students with the curriculum that we were taking because of the seriousness of some of the emotional needs that they knew we would have to face. This helped to navigate my emotions toward more positivity and build my self esteem. A number of the walls of dysfunction that plagued my life were slowly being torn down.

God always has a way to look after each of us. Our trials and tribulations are building blocks of the compass that navigates the road to our destiny. My grade point average stayed at 4.0 and above. Determination increased more and more to succeed and obtain each of my goals.

Prior to graduation, an investor came to the school and approached me regarding my future and what I planned to do with the education once I graduated.

He set up a number of additional brain storming meetings as he finalized various proposals. His plans were to build a safe haven home for young women who had experienced all the trauma that occurred in my life. This was truly a miracle that was not expected.

After several meetings, he immediately went to work on the project. Within a matter of months an architect had presented renderings of the building, rooms,

and recreational areas. The home was built with state of the art equipment and applications were being taken for hiring staff so that they would be in place when the ribbon would be cut at the grand opening.
He called me to schedule another meeting to present the proposal of me heading up the project at the home.

I was shocked, amazed, and happy all at the same time; was this a dream I kept asking myself. All types of thoughts started to flood my brain as I relived the conversation but I didn't have any money to support a project this large at the moment. This project was huge and would take quite a large of mount of money to fund.

The investor was looking for some one with passion about helping and rescuing young women who had been victimized and marred for life; He wanted to hire a person to head the project with the same compassion that he felt in his heart. He assured me that I didn't need any money. In fact he offered me a salary that seemed beyond belief. This would afford me the opportunity to get an apartment, move my sister with me, pay for her education and give a better quality of life. As time went on, we became very good friends. Little by little he began to build the trust in men that I lost. My concept of all men being dogs began to change. He was a perfect gentlemen, warm, kind, compassionate and very professional. His college friends labeled him as a nerd. I didn't care about what they labeled him; It was like a breath of fresh air to know and meet a man with such integrity.

He insisted that I have a corner office that was decorated by the best designers in their field. Had my vision board become a reality? Wow, I was in a good place emotionally and did not want to leave.

He shared thoughts and ideas regarding the girls home and asked for my input before making any final decisions; we made a perfect team. All the bitterness, anger, and concept that all men are dogs began to dissipate and fade away.

Excitement filled my heart as looked for an apartment for my sister and I . Finding the perfect warm and cozy place was now removed from my to do list. Shortly after my sister came to live with me, our mother passed away leaving our father alone.

Neither my sister or I wanted to go back to ever visit the horrible home we left. However, both of us prayed to forgive our father for all the awful things that he had done to us as well as put our mother through. She was now resting in peace, out of pain and misery that she suffered from the injuries of the accident..We often wondered if she knew what our father was doing to us.

This Fox that entered our home and heart had been put out. What a relief; Light was now at the end of the tunnel and shining very brightly. Thanks be unto God !!!!!!

Everything was going extremely well. Eunice now started to walk down memory lane and looked through the mirror of what she had come out of.
Eunice grew up in a home with both a toxic mother and father who came from toxic homes. There was never kind or positive words between any of them. They enjoyed picking one another apart with every cruel word or name that they could think of.

Her mother would always criticize every parent in the neighborhood and always had something negative to say about every family and their children. My mother seemed like she almost hated herself and her personality showed it. She felt that she was
always being watched, and judged. Her appearance was horrible and it was pasted on to each one of our family members everyone else was so well groomed.

My wardrobe changed drastically once I entered college. It was like stepping into a completely different era. Fashion and styles became a part of the daily routine. Prior to that we looked like we were dressed for a Halloween party.

Life was finally better for my sister and I. Emotional balance plays a big part of our well being, performance, and our temperament. It was a though we both had come out of a tunnel of horror and a haunted house.

We received an overwhelming number of applications and the girls home was filled to capacity within less than a week.

The staff went to work immediately placing each applicant and ensuring each one of them of the safety that the home provided.

After a year's time we noticed that the girls had made wonderful strides of improvement their emotional healing, self confidence, and self validation.

Anthony the wonderful man that made all this happen and I went out to one of our favorite restaurants to celebrate our accomplishment of all the wonderful team work that had been put into the project.

While at the dinner table, Something happened that blew me totally away. He proposed to me presenting me with this beautiful engagement ring asking if I would make him the happiest man on earth by spending the rest of my life with him.

In total shock, I asked him if I could think about it. Well, I didn't think to long; We were married six months later. The wedding was absolutely beautiful. Something that I never dreamed of in my entire life.
I never thought I would ever be happy. God had a different direction and plan for my sister and I. I couldn't have been happier. As we partnered at the Safe Haven home, that home turned into three locations.

We were able to change the lives of a countless number of children and young women. My sister went on to finish college and is a successful entrepreneur.

The fox entered our lives but was destroyed. The fox does not have to destroy your lives or kill you !!!!!
You can kill him !!!!

The Fox of Toxic Relationships

According to dictionary.com toxic is defined as causing unpleasant feelings; harmful or malicious: acting as or having the effect of poison. This chapter speaks and identifies toxic relationships which can harm and even kill you if you become victimized with that type or those types of people without escaping.

One of the dangers of negativity is that it impacts not only the mind but the emotions. There are a number of day cares experiencing this type of behavior with the toddlers that they care for . If you have ever observed toddlers playing, have you ever noticed how they are attracted to a certain group? As time goes on, there are children that love to inflict pain on others. They walk around bitting and hitting the other children. Some of them take their toys and use them as weapons.

If this behavior is not corrected or dealt with, It will mushroom into bitterness, and negativity. Some parents make the mistake of showing favoritism among siblings, laugh and think that this is cute but they are creating a monster; not realizing that this will cause friction among the siblings and peers resulting in bad behavior that could follow them through out their lives. A number of them become bullies loving to inflict pain on others as they become school age and go through life. Unfortunately it does not stop unless it is corrected.

The bullies go after the one who is the weakest link. His or her goal is to make the individual feel less than with a number demeaning gestures. Inflicting pain on others gives these individuals a sense of importance. They feel validated with a place of control.

Matt and Julie were neighbors who moved into the neighborhood during the the summer break as the school year was ending. But neither he or his wife had any children. He seemed to be polite with a mild mattered sort of personality so we thought.

His wife was very quiet and didn't have much to say about anything. She always spoke to the neighbors with a loving gentle smile.

Matt was extremely passive aggressive. One of his vices was over indulging in alcohol. He could never defend himself in any type of confrontation unless he had a couple of drinks to boost his ego. The alcohol seemed to give him courage to say what ever was on his mind.

Additionally, he was very insecure with some what of a low self esteem. He had a habit of always accusing people of mistreating him including his wife.
One holiday weekend our neighborhood was in for a horrible horrific day. Matt had been binging on alcohol all week end ranting and raging over minuscule meaningless subjects.

In an effort to escape the madness in the house, Julie left the house to get a break. The constant nagging had become unbearable.

When he noticed that she had left, he questioned all the children who were outside playing. Grilling each one of them of her where a-bouts. Rather than drive, he walked for blocks and blocks looking for Julie who just needed a break.

The longer he walked not seeing her, the madder he became. Anger and rage bubbled up in his heart like a soda that was fizzing. He felt that he no longer had control of his marriage and his home. How could his wife leave the house without even telling him where she was going? Not with standing that he had emotional abused her through out the entire night.

Julie was emotionally worn out from all that had transpired through out the night. The hours away from the house was calm, peaceful, and allowed her to gather her thoughts without being verbally abused, used as a punching bag, and called names.

When Julie returned, he screamed and screamed demanding to know where she had been for the hours away from the house. He grabbed a bottle from the off the table and hit her in the head with a bottle which broke causing cuts through out her scalp. Enraged he pushed and punched her repeatedly with uncontrollable anger. Traumatized and shocked by the blood that ran from her head down her face, she saw what looked like a mad man who was totally out of control. Who is this beast that she married she asked herself?

Prior to their marriage, it seemed like this union was going to be perfect. How wrong I was thinking that my marriage was going to be for life. As tears mixed with blood ran down her face she tried not to scream hysterically but sobbed quietly.

The paramedics were called by a neighbor who heard the commotion and she was rushed to the hospital which resulted in 25 stitches. The police made a report of the incident and was ordered to go to her house and talk to her husband. He was asked to leave the home for the remainder of the weekend to sober up and cool off.

The men of the neighborhood had a meeting and concluded that Matt needed help. They never thought or imagined that he was such a monster. The meeting concluded with the fact women who are the weaker vessel and are to be treated with love, care and very delicately. The committee members of the block vowed to ensure that Matt got the help he needed.

Truly this was a toxic relationship; like the poison venom that comes from a poisonous snake bite. She was accused of meeting another man, that was not the case at all. She needed a break ; as she walked through the neighborhood which gave her a sense of calmness that helped her to release everything that transpired all night long.

After he returned home, he cried begging for her forgiveness saying that this would never happen again. As he held her in his arms telling her how much he loved her and was so very sorry for flying off the handle in the matter that he did, she kept thinking if this would really be the last time or would it escalate by her losing her life the next time around.

Why did he have a concept of always thinking that everyone was out to get him? This level of insecurity causes detrimental circumstances.

No one knew what his home life was like while he was growing up. But the truth of the matter is that he grew up in a home of violence and dysfunction. This dark cloud of shame was a secret that he never wanted to talk about or address because of how ugly and miserable things were. He wanted this to be locked away and never be revealed to anyone.

When he and Julie got married his parents were both deceased and the subject of home life was never discussed.

The next few months seemed to be going very smoothly. The scars on her head were healing but my scars in my heart will remain for life.
I grew up in foster care with two loving parents who displayed nothing but love and appreciation for one another as she was being interviewed by a social worker.

There were triggers that ignited the violent behavior that Matt had that I was not aware of but constantly walked around like there were egg shells through out the house to try to ensure that there were no explosions.

Blaming myself, I went to see a therapist and explained everything that happened with each incident who assured me that I was not the problem. Matt was really the one who needed therapy. He had major problems that needed attention. But he refused to go and get any type of help; he kept saying that there wasn't anything wrong with him.

The therapist advised me to leave before things got worse or become deadly. He arranged for me to stay at a safe house for battered women where Matt would not be able to find me. Being up rooted was a bit of an adjustment but I feared for my life and proceeded with the move.

My love for Matt was what kept me in that toxic relationship as long as it did. I packed a little at a time preparing for the move so there would no suspicion of my move.

Can you imagine how it felt not to be nervous every day of your life or afraid to even breath hard for fear of being beaten to a pulp.

The day that I left seemed as though the sun was shining brighter than ever. The new chapter in my life was beginning after being in the safe house. A new journey traveling the road of my destiny was starting to unfold. Each day became brighter and brighter.

I could sleep at night without fear of being awaken by being punched or getting blows to my head. What sense of safety of knowing that I wouldn't be pushed out of the bed on to the floor or raped by my husband.

I could think clearly and finally discovered who I really was. The scars and bruises were still there but my love for Matt never died. I regretted that things turned out for us the way that they did. But my life was more important than staying in a relationship that got worse by the day.

Matt never went to get any help. He thought that everyone needed help but him. He told the neighbors that I was in desperate need of help. Months later I learned through the social worker that he was sick. I truly felt sorry for him and didn't wish any thing bad for him.

A few years later he had passed away from cancer all alone with out any one by his side; which freed my life totally from fear and emotional bondage that I had lived with for years. Finally, no more hiding, no more fear, and no more running away from Matt.

What makes life beat you to a pulp? Warnings signs should never be taken for granted or ignored . Before marriage it is important to see if there are any signs of mental illness in the life or family of the man that you want to spend the rest of your life with, violence, and or dysfunction. Once this information has been attained, please don't ignore the warning signs. Avoid every effort not to let a fox like this come into your home or heart.

Toxic relationships can be with a person who you thought was a friend but found out that he or she was negative, envious, jealous, and loves sabotage. This fox can also be lurking in the work place where you may be surrounded by saboteurs who are vicious and evil who do anything to ruin their neighbors, coworkers, or families's reputation . This group of people seem to have a heart that is callous and love to inflict pain or see others suffer.

Choose your friends wisely; observe the attitude and behavior of those who you let in your personal space. Don't be afraid to sever the relationship without any remorse.

This is for your own GOOD!!!! Please be aware.

The Fox of Fear

This fox has torment and can cause harm, hurt, both physically and emotionally.

Tina grew up living in fear from the time she was five years old. Her older siblings would locked her up in a dark room or a closet and say that the bookie man was coming to get her. She would cry for hours begging them to let her out of the dark closet. But listening to her sobs seemed amusing to them but they had no idea of the affect that this had on her.

They threatened to even beat her if she told their parents what was going on. This went on for years causing bed wetting, nervousness, and an extreme amount of fear.

The fear carried over into her teen age years . This resulted in doubt and insecurity to start or finish any projects. If a project would be started she would be gripped with so much fear of being a failure until nothing would be accomplished. She became an emotional wreck with each new venture starting and stopping but never completing anything.

The fear of failure resulted in her not getting jobs done that she was more than qualified to do. But there was little or no confidence to be had which made life a little unbearable.

As child it was bed wetting, but now there were panic attacks, nervousness, and a feeling of being stuck in a position with no means of escape or moving forward.

She was extremely talented, warmed hearted with magnetism that caused any body that she came in contact with to become motivated to reach for and obtain their goals.

One of her other attributes was that she was an outstanding public speaker that captivated every audience that had the opportunity of ever hearing her speak.

The words seem to roll off her tongue leaving her listeners mesmerized with a desire to want to do better moving full throttle into a higher level of learning , goal setting, or career building. She had to get free from this awful plight.

As time went on, being disgusted with how her life was going, she enrolled in a number of classes and seminars that made a complete turn around from her childhood trauma. She had to get over this fear that gripped her like a ball and chain.

Would she ever be free? This was such a big hindrance in her life that slowed down her progress of achieving goals for a long time. Although she managed to cover it up while speaking to a group of people or with her colleagues the fact still remained that she was going to fight this fox and win the battle.

Today she stands tall as a confident successful business woman and phenomenal motivational speaker.

The Fox of Counterfeit Love

According to dictionary.com counterfeit is something made in exact imitation of something valuable or important with the intention to deceive or defraud. Have you ever been deceived?

Everyone is looking for love., kind words, accolades, and an emotional safe place. As children are born into the world there are a number of things that happens, each child experiences touch, taste, feel, and smell ETC.
The embrace of a mother warms and gives her baby comfort, love, and a sense of safety as well as protection .

As children grow into adulthood , they look for true love. Unfortunately, sometimes they look for love in all the wrong places or are deceived about what true love is leading them down a path of falling into a pit of a cycle that could go on for generations.

There are a number of women who mistake sex for true love. Sex was designed by God for a married man and woman to share in a beautiful blissful experience satisfying each other intimately to the highest degree.

However, the fox of counterfeit love has taken the beauty out of such a union. He has destroyed the sanctity of marriage and instituted a mental concept into the hearts and minds of many that believe that marriage is a farce and a thing of the past.

They feel that in order to see if the man that they are with is compatible, or if they are a match for each other; They enter into a syndrome called playing house.

This entails doing everything a married couple would do like making a purchase of a house, car, furniture, obtaining an apartment and etc. In the absence of vows before God and people as well as a legal marriage license.

This concept has destroyed the futures of a number of women and their children. Pushing them in a category where they never know or experience true love.

Sex is not love. Many use the word " I Love You" very loosely. A Man will tell a woman that the loves her just to engage in sexual intercourse. Using her as a method to bring pleasure to himself. Once the encounter is over he moves to the next woman and tells her the same thing.

They also use some women to help them attain good credit, a home cooked meal, a fancy wardrobe, a better job, and clout among their friends and peers.

God has especially designed ever woman in His beautiful garden full of gifts, talents, and abilities. He has given her a number of emotional strengthens that aren't present in men. She has been designed to have enormous emotional strength. She had the ability to weather a number of emotional storms that men can't handle.

On the other hand some women are mis guided to think that if that have a baby for a man that this will be the glue that keeps him in their lives. This is an illusion, but I am sorry to say that he will leave you baby and all; especially if he is tired of you because there is no true love there . Some men enter into counterfeit love as a means of mere convenience of a built in maid or cook.

There is a scripture in the bible that says: Love is long-suffering and is kind. **1 Corinthians 13:4-8**

KJV allows us to look into the mirror of reality about true love.

Having a child will not be the glue at all; in fact, If this concept is not stopped or corrected, women will end up with children for a number of different fathers. Each Counterfeit love relationship encountered takes a piece of emotion away from you. In some cases a piece of you dies, is crippled, and changes you into a different person.

Just think, each one of the children conceived and is born into any of these relationships will come into the world with emotional disorders or some sort of problem. Some get to know their biological fathers and some don't. Additionally, the children are abused, taunted, and constantly reminded that he or she is just like the father that walked out of their lives. Sadly, the product of counterfeit love results in so many things; sibling rivalry enters into the picture causing resentment, jealousy, and wounds that may never go away.

Children become insecure wondering where they belong or who that really belong to.

Baby mama drama in almost every case comes into the picture where the children witness arguing, fighting, rejection, abandonment, and unnecessary violence. A war of competition between the women involved result in cat fights, bitterness, resentment, and revenge that becomes a great concern to try to pay the individuals back to try to make them hurt as bad as you have were.

Please understand that you can never pay any body back for the hurt and pain that you were put through or endured.
On many occasions that revenge turns into a poison spewing out like a venomous snake that only causes more damage, destruction, and sometimes even death.

The absence of men from the homes have caused so much havoc in a number of families.

Women don't know how to train their sons. A woman cannot train a man how to be a man. It takes a man to do that, So, boys that grow up in homes with the absence of a father have no clue of how to be men. They lack social skills of what to do and how to treat a woman. There is no knowledge of what their role as head of household entails. Not realizing that they are suppose to be priest, protector, and provider of the home which gives their sons an example to follow as they grow into their adult life.

Men end up growing into manhood with the mentally of a small boy totally immature. Like the women that they connect with, the relationship always ends up being counterfeit love because they don't know how or what real love is all about. Many of them go in and out of relationships like revolving doors keeping a score how many women they can be involved with. It is like playing a game of monopoly or scrabble; life to them is like one big game.

Women with the same attitude trade in men like they are purchasing a new car. Unfortunately, the poor children of these relationships suffer and the cycle goes on and on. It is a generational curse with a cycle that should and must be broken.

How can this cycle be stopped? Women remember that you are a beautiful flower divinely arrayed as one of God's beautiful flowers with a journey and destiny to be fulfilled while on earth.

Your value and worth is more than being a toy or puppet for some one who doesn't care or really love you. You don't need to be validated by entering into counterfeit love relationships. First, Love your self and seek to find your purpose with the gifting that you possess. Avoid listening to fair weather friends who are negative and saboteurs who are full of jealousy and envy who feed only on confusion as though it were an after dinner delight.

Get into programs that are designed only to make you a better person, lift up your self esteem, believe in yourself, surround yourself with positive people .

Look for qualities in a man who doesn't want to use you for his personal gain. Learn to ask questions and take personal surveys such as the following:

- Does he have a job
- Is he depending on your salary for support
- Is he kind, gentle, and a gentleman
- What are his goals and objectives for the next five years and beyond
- Is he and his family mentally stable
- What about his integrity
- Does he know how to communicate
- Does he know how to engage in a conversation without talking at you
- Does he scream and use abusive tones or language when having a conversation
- Is he a physical or verbal abuser
- Does he fly off the handle quickly
- Are there minor things that trigger his temper to a boiling point
- Always look for red flags
- What type of home life did he have with his parents
- Does he own a car
- Does he manage his finances well
- Does he look out for your interest

- Does he have his own house or apartment
- Does he act extra in the presence of others
- Is he a bragger
- Is he insensitive
- Is everything always about him
- Is he sensitive to the needs of others

Accept the truth about the individual if he is a flake. Don't make excuses to justify being with him. You deserve better.

If you are entrapped in a counterfeit love relationship, struggling to be free, run for your life. Look for resources that help women with children in this situation. Be determined to escape and look for a better way of life. Life doesn't have to filled with misery but it can be blissful with the right partner.

Please don't become entrapped with this fox!!!!!

The Fox of Dysfunction

Dysfunction is an abnormal behavior . It is an abnormal fox. Those involved often consider themselves as being normal because there isn't any thing else the individual or family knows to compare to. It is often fueled by ignorance, violence, drugs, alcohol abuse, and emotional trauma .

Let's discuss dysfunction :

The Byrd family seemed like an ordinary family who lived in a middle class community. However, the were at the height of being dysfunctional. They thought that name calling, fighting, and physical abuse was normal. They had two sons who were tainted by this behavior. When they started dating Not only was this behavior exercised in their family but they treated everyone that they came in contact with the same way.

They were bullies that thought that they were superior to any and every one they came in contact with. What a misconception of life.

There was not any evidence of love, care, or sensitivity but they thought that this was normal.

The school made several calls about their sons bad behavior to their parents almost every week about fights, name calling to other students and harassment in several of their classes.

Poor Mrs. Byrd!!! She was very kind, warn and very soft spoken. Her husband Bruce had no lines of communication with her at all. He'd rather physically abuse her than engage in a decent conversation.
He used her as a punching bag if anything went wrong on his job or in the home which was his way releasing the anxiety he felt.

She kept hoping that things would get better and he would change his way of living. Instead, He became more violent towards her. She Isolated herself from all of her friends but a neighbor who she talk to in confidence regarding the miserable home life.

Their sons and their friends acted just like their father going about terrorizing the neighborhood. Between her husband and their sons, the worry got to be just too much to bear.

To make things even worse, her youngest son became addicted to drugs that would numb the emotional pain of what was going on in his family.

The appetite for the drugs grew larger and larger as he watched his father abuse his mother week after week.. He refused to seek help or share the trauma he endured ; Over a period of a year all his veins started to collapse from the use of heroine. When that happened he used the veins in his eyes to get high. After they collapsed, he moved to his private parts.

Mrs. Byrd had become extremely depressed.   Can you imagine a mother watch her child destroy him or herself. She just wanted to end it all and pondered over what she was going to do to make that happen..

As the months passed, she decided that she couldn't take it any more. She was tired of sleepless nights crying and crying all night and trying to reason with both her husband and her sons. Matters seemed to be getting worse and worse. Nothing that she did or said seemed to be a remedy to the problem.

Depression had pushed her to the limit of enduring the abuse that seemed to be her punishment every day. Would it ever end?

For months she pondered over and over of how , when, and where , she could end this awful married life. Her husband acted like a brute beast of a man, her children were out of control and there was never peace in the home. The children had virtually no respect for her as their mother which broke her heart .

A clean house or warm prepared meals meant nothing to those ungrateful people in my home she cried as her tear stained pillow became wet from the emotional pain and anguish she suffered.

Everyone in her home just took all her efforts for granted. Her sons felt entitled to get what ever that wanted and thought that she should be at their every beck and call.

When she attempted to ask her husband's family to speak with him to see if that would help, war swept through her house like a destructive tornado; this meant that she would be beaten and called names for days for reaching out for help.

Was it really worth it to approach his family for help she asked? Reaching out to whomever or what ever would bring peace in her home was her objective.

Would there ever be any peace? She was labeled as a whiner.

There was no where to go or no one to turn to that could get her the help she needed. Suicidal thoughts raced through her mind non stop.

All sorts of questions flashed one by one like lighten bolts asking her what was her purpose in life , what was she living for, and why didn't she prepare to end her pain and suffering. The question was how!!!!!

As time went on she decided that there was no other way out but to take her life to end it all. The fighting, physical abuse, constant rejection from the family would be a thing of the past.
besides who could she really reach out to for help? Bruce's family refused to even try to deal with the issues that were at hand, her only half sister would only reach out to Bruce which meant that he would come and get her, demand that she return home, punish her with multiple beatings every day.

As she pondered, the more she was convinced that this would be the only way to make Bruce and her sons would feel an enormous amount of pain and end the pain she endured everyday. After all, look at how they treated her day in and day out.

Suicide is something that hurts the family, loved ones and friends of those who engage in this exercise. There had to be other options that crossed her mind but each time they did, she thought of a million and one reasons why none of them would work.

If she ran away, where would she go? How would she support herself? where or who would she stay with?

Day after day she began to isolate herself more and more. Going into isolation was the worse thing that could have happened. While being isolated all sort of negative things kept coming to mind as the strategy to take her life was being planned .

After being locked in the dark basement for three days with out food or water, when Bruce finally unlocked the door as he left for work, walking in a daze and crying uncontrollably, She decided that this would be the last time she would ever go through any more physical or emotional abuse.

She made her way to a near by freeway. As horns honked and head lights flashed, she kept walking into incoming traffic that was going a record speed.

There was no way that the driver could stop. She was killed instantly from the impact. The noise and smell of brakes filled the air. Traffic was backed up for miles as several cars plowed into each other. Helicopter police radioed and had officers on the ground dispatch traffic police, ambulances, hazmat and sadly to say the coroner.

People got out of their cars to see what happened, traffic was backed up for miles until an assessment of the incident was investigated.

The driver who hit her was on his way home from work with thoughts of enjoying a special dinner that his wife had prepared for their date night. Needless to say, that he didn't happen. Devastated and in total shock he kept reliving that awful incident with thoughts of how it might have been avoided. But there was no way that he could have avoided hitting her.

Action news was on the scene as other news media groups arrived. Yes !!!! you guessed it. He had to go to therapy for over a year.

A breaking news flash reported that a woman was killed by a car hitting and killing her on the freeway. Jaws dropped and tears flowed form the eyes of almost everyone who heard the tragic story. Many wondered how could this have even happened. A number of women tried to analyze every aspect of how she got to the freeway and was able to walk into incoming traffic. They made up their own details before getting the true story as people who gossip do.

It's amazing how they add and subject without knowing the true facts.

The entire neighborhood was sadden to hear that this was someone that they knew. The news media said that this woman went to a near by freeway and walked into on coming traffic and was killed instantly from the impact. Her little mangled body was scattered over several traffic lanes. The people that had to bag the body and take it to the morgue were in tears as they picked up each part of her little body.

Two policeman came to the home of the deceased to inform the family of the tragedy. They were able to determine who it was by the identification they found in her purse. Prior to leaving home, she made sure that she had identification in her purse.

When her family heard the news they were overwhelmed and fell to their knees in grief and despair. Her husband Bruce screamed, his knees buckled, and cried like a wounded animal as he fell to the floor. He kept saying that it was all his fault and blamed himself thinking of all the wrong he had ever done. Every beating that he ever gave her starred him in the face like a video being played over and over.

The youngest son Tim called his father names and left the house in a rage to find the nearest drug dealer. He couldn't put enough drugs in his system to try to numb the pain of losing his mother. The oldest son Stan starred into space for hours at the time wondering what he could have done different to save his mother's life or treat her better.

He thought of all the times he disrespected her, refused to obey any of her instructions, and called her names, and got into trouble at school.

The house reeked with the smell of death, grief, and sadness. Neighbors came over and brought food trying to console the family as much as they could.

The trash was filled with boxes and boxes of tissue from all the tears that flowed from that day and several others.

Words cannot describe the grief that each of the family members felt or expressed. The television and radio was not turned on for weeks because the horrible description of what happened haunted them enough without any added pressure. The news media repeated the story over and over for days.

There was only fragments of her body left. As a result the mortician suggested that cremation of her remains would be best.

Planning the memorial service was extremely hard on her husband. He had married a sweet, naive, loving young girl who only wanted love and happiness and to return it to her family.

A doctor had to be present to administer something to keep the family calm during the process of making the funeral arrangements.

The funeral was very sad and the neighbors cried and mourned for months. She should have left him they all proclaimed and maybe she would be alive today was the conversation on the lips of ever one in the neighborhood.

As for her children, life went on but it was very difficult. With the absence of a kind, loving, and warm mother was heart breaking for each of them. Her husband Bruce lived a life of regret and began to drink more and more.

His doctor suggested that he take up a hobby to help take his mind off the situation and reduce the intake of so much alcohol .

He took up a hunting sport with a friend of many years to try to release the frustration and grief that he encountered on a daily basis. His conscience beat him up every day non stop. He kept seeing her preparing home cooked meals for the family and thinking of how the aroma of freshly baked apple pie would meet him at the door as he entered the house from work. He wished over and over that he would have been a better person and most of all a better husband.

Year after year he visited the grave site where her ashes were buried and lay prostrate crying uncontrollably and screaming her name to the top of his lungs saying how sorry he was and asking for her forgiveness but it was too late.
Bruce watched the door every day for hours looking for his wife who would never enter that door again in his life time.

He clung to the blanket where she sleep every night smelling the aroma of her body scent and refused to wash it.

He suffered from night mares of which he visualized his wife being hit and killed by the on coming traffic on that freeway.

Riddled with guilt, Bruce realized that his sweet, warm, and loving wife and mother of his children was never coming back. Months later, with many sleepless nights, which caused his health to deteriorate, the family doctor recommended that he see a therapist and attend grief counseling sessions.

This helped tremendously but never took away the pain of how he felt responsible for this whole horrific night mare. He wished that all this was a bad dream and he would wake up and everything would be back to normal.

After a year of therapy he encouraged his youngest son to get treatment for his drug addiction for fear of losing him to a drug over dose.

After thinking about what a mess his life was in and getting worse by the day. Tim decided to go for help. He had lost a lot of weight and his health was on the decline just like his father's.

The doctor explained that this was a long hard journey because the drugs stay in your system for a least five years. He explained that determination was an important factor in becoming drug free. Additionally, he let him know that the treatment was going to be done by weaning him off the drugs because cold turkey might have killed him. It was not an easy journey but he persevered. Pain ripped through his body like hundreds of knives were stabbing him all at the same time. The craving for more drugs was worse than a pregnant woman craving for foods during her pregnancy.

He had to be placed in a facility that specializes in the recovery of addictions ; because there was absolutely no way that he could do this as an out patient. For weeks he was not allowed to see or contact his brother or father while going through the worse part of his recovery.

When the human body is abused from substance abuse there is a day by day determination that the patient has to keep to the fore front of his or her mind.

After looking at his fragile body and all the damage that the drugs had done that was more than enough to help him make up his mind to recover.

It eventually paid off, his son successfully went through rehabilitation and after six months he began to look better . He was beginning to gain his weight back. The color came back into his skin. He didn't look like he was going to die at any minute. Day by day the son started his road to continue his road to recovery. How ever, the price for using those drugs cost him some serious health challenges ; a number collapsed veins, arthritis was in almost all of his joints from sleeping on cold sidewalks and in crack houses without heat or running water. Selling his shoes and walking barefooted just to get high just to name a few. Yes!!! the price paid for his a addiction was not cheap but very costly.

What causes dysfunction and how can we escape that tragedy that comes with it. How can we become aware that our life and home is in a dysfunctional state.

Education plays a major role in awareness. If you are Living in what is called your own little bubble of life without exploring other cultures, ways of living, and a positive life style it can be dangerous. Surround your self with only positive people, accepting the fact that Toxic people are like terminal incurable cancer dangerous to your well being and if the ties are not severed ; they will kill you physically or emotionally.

It is important to self evaluate and do something about your findings without making false promises or excuses to your self about change. Love yourself enough to Change!!!! You can do it. What ever you do , don't procrastinate. Get the fox out of your house.!!!!!!!! in fact, make a point of never to let him enter .

The Fox of Bitterness

Bitterness is a fox that has destroyed so many lives. In a number of cases this starts off being very small and mushrooms into a root that loges itself intwining itself like a vine in the depths of the heart. This fox is cruel , cunning, and determines to separate, and drive the individual to complete madness on a quest to destroy him or her.

Dictionary definition .com gives a clear picture of what bitterness is and what it can do. Bitterness causes anger and disappointment and an individual to be treated unfairly. It is synonymous with resentment and envy.

Let's look a little deeper into what bitterness does. According to the KJV bible dictionary it causes Sharpness; severity of temper. Sharp, words, reproachful; sarcastic.

Thanksgiving day had finally arrived; this day was very special in the home of the Carrs family. The girls assisted their mother in the preparation of this day that everyone looked forward to every year.

Mrs. Carr started shopping for days and storing everything on the menu to ensure that there was enough for everyone to enjoy.

She always had the daughters help her chop, cut, slice, grate, and bake.

Each sibling had a specific job to make the day festive and enjoyable. The teen agers were in charge of games of which they always made them exciting.

The smaller children colored and played games on their smart phones.
The table was set with the best of linen, fine china, and stem ware. Our mother was insulted if any paper plates and cutlery was used on that day. Her linen table cloths were removed from the boxes that the cleaners had so neatly prepared them for storage. Excitement was in the air because the family always had such a good time at these holiday celebrations.

As the guest arrived, everyone assembled in the family room. Cameras were set in place to capture the best poses of all the family members upon entering. Before the family was called to be seated sat the dinning room table, the women shared stories of bargains at the malls, the latest fashion, and new hair styles they had been introduced to by their hair stylist.

While the men bragged about the latest basket ball team and who had won the championship with little or no effort ; on the other hand Grandparents displayed pictures of each of their grandchildren from birth to their present age sharing expressions of how proud they were that the lineage of the family would continue to grow.

Each family member as well as invited guest had to give reasons why he or she was thankful for all the blessings they received through out the year. Afterwards everyone was to be seated at the dinning room table and prepare for dinner. The meal was a sight to behold. Every thing was arrayed on the table like nothing we had ever seen and looked like something out a Better Homes and Garden magazine.

As the dinner music played softly in the background, all of a sudden the atmosphere of the room changed drastically. A cousin who hadn't attended the family dinners or gatherings for years was ringing the door bell.

It was our Cousin Reggie at the family thanksgiving dinner, everyone was in total shock; we hadn't seen him in years. Everyone looked at each other in amazement hoping that there wouldn't be any altercation between him and our uncle George.

Uncle George who was the head of the house had stepped away for a brief moment. While he was gone, Reggie took the liberty of sitting at the head of the table without question. Upon his return all eyes were focused on him wondering what his reaction would be when he saw cousin Reggie. He took one look at Reggie and his facial expression changed. It was the image of a snorting bull in a ring with his matador.

Then in a matter of minutes a major war broke out in the dining room. Cousin Reggie made the mistake of sitting at the head of the table where uncle George who was head of the house always sat. George took pride in sitting in that seat and counted it an honor to always sit there. This made him feel important not only to his wife and kids but to the entire family. This gave him a sense of pride to be labeled as Priest, Protector, and Provider of his household. The family looked up to uncle George for all his accomplishments, encouragements to all the young men, and the help he provided for those who couldn't afford to pay their college tuition or became short on their rent payment and lack enough money to buy food.

He was also a mentor to a number of people on his job before he retired. But seeing cousin Reggie was a trigger that we hated to see and hoped that this would not escalate in to something that he would be sorry for. It was such a beautiful day and a lovely occasion. We had brought our appetites, set our eyes on what dishes we were going to be trying, everyone had his or her Tupperware ready to take home a plate for a late night snack. You guessed it!!!! Things suddenly change.

For some reason, uncle George was on edge and became enraged. All the anger, bitterness, and the resentment he ever felt towards Reggie escalated to the highest level ever seen before.

Uncle George resented cousin Reggie for years. He just couldn't seem to find a place in his heart to forgive him . There had been a confrontation between the two of them over some mis management of money that cost uncle George to loose a large client in his business. Reggie worked in his office as a an accounting controller. Poor choices put this flow of bad blood between the two of them when he messed up the accounting with some bad investments for one of his best clients.

Uncle George never forgave him and roots of bitterness began to grow in his heart against Reggie more and more. No matter how many apologies Reggie gave him it was never enough to erase the injustice that he felt. The very site of Reggie disgusted him and set his heart into a burning inferno. The wound, hurt, and disappointment began to fester more and more and deepen like an open sore that seems like it will never heal. Why couldn't he let it go?

Things escalated more on a day the family thought that the holiday would bring about a change and this awful attitude would leave. However, that wasn't the case.

All Uncle George could seem to think about was that fact he lost a large sum of money and a good client. The anger turned to bitterness and a dangerous rage. When he returned to the dinning room, he pulled Reggie from the table striking him a carving knife. A huge fight between the two of them broke out right there in the dinning room. Reggie was stabbed multiple times.

This wonderful day turned into a tragic end. Reggie was fatally stabbed multiple times , the doctors did all they could to save him but despite the blood transfusions he had lost a lot of blood and died on the operating table.

The entire family was sitting in the waiting room of the hospital when the doctor came out of the operating room with the grim news that their cousin was dead. How could something like this happen on such as special day fell from the lips of each relative.

Nothing in the house could be moved. The police came and took everything that was evidence from the house. Their report stated that this was a murder. We were all asked not to leave the state or country because there was going to be questioning so that they could present the evidence in court. In fact, all of us were summoned to court at the hearing and trial.

Uncle George came to himself and began to think rationally, as to whether this root of bitterness could have been avoided. Yes, it was true that Reggie costed him a client, a friend, and a large sum of money. But now uncle George's life was ruined forever and would never be the same as a result of the fox of bitterness. His family was separated, the family dinners became a thing of the past, his marriage was on the rocks, Reggie's family was absent of a husband and a father.

Uncle George had not only made a complete spectacle of himself but allowed the fox of bitterness to ruin the lives of so many family members as well as his own.

The news media and talk shows couldn't stop talking about the man who was booked for murder because his cousin sat at the head of the table at the family at theThanks giving dinner. They went on to say that a man was carved instead of the turkey.

Was that a reason to allow his anger to result in murder?

The bible is a lamp unto our feet, a guide for direction and acts as a compass to lead us the right way. According to **Ephesians 4: 26-27 NLT** It is not a sin to be angry but when it feasters and grows it becomes a deadly poison that can result in death.

And don't sin by letting anger control you. Don't let the sun go down while you are still angry, anger gives a foot hold to the devil.

Prior to this incident Uncle George was never a person who showed any characteristics of being a violent man. The family always complimented him on how he was always able to defuse scraps and fights among family members. This whole fiscal was so different then times in the past.

Everyone could not get over the shock of what happened at the Thanksgiving dinner.

He will have to spend the rest of his life in prison because failure to defuse the anger had turned into the ugly fox of bitterness.

As the family returned from the hospital, the appetites of everyone had vanished. Did we really feel like eating anything ? The shock of Reggie being dead and uncle George being booked for murder was very heart wrenching. Tears flowed for hours as they relived the struggle that seemed like a script from a movie.

After the trial he was sentenced to life in prison without ever being approved for any type of parole.

Did it have to go that far? As we ponder over things that upset us or cause us to become angry, we must never cross the line that causes us to want to harm or pay the individual back.

Vengeance does not belong to us. God will reward every man or woman for everything that he or she has ever done. Father time always has a way of collecting more than what we can imagine. Look at what the fox of bitterness did to uncle George. He lost his marriage, his family, and his very life as he sits in a prison cell stripped of everything that ever mattered to him.

Please I beg of you, don't let the fox of bitterness destroy you !!!!!!!!!!!

The Fox of Deep Depression

This fox loves isolation of his victims. He does everything to keep his victims away from family and friends or any one that can help them out of this deep depression.
The Isolation pushes the individuals into a dark place emotionally. Rosa Brown a beautiful talented young woman fell victim to the fox of deep depression.

According to Merriam Webster Dictionary, depression is a state of feeling sad in low spirits, melancholy; *specifically* : A **mood disorder** that is marked by varying degrees of sadness, despair, and loneliness, and that is typically accompanied by inactivity, guilt, loss of concentration, social withdrawal, sleep disturbances, and sometimes suicidal tendencies.

The following are some Signs of Depression

- Having trouble concentrating, thinking or making decisions.
- Feeling like you are in a fog
- Having thoughts of suicide
- Loss of energy
- Feeling lethargic
- Feeling worthless or less than
- Trouble sleeping
- Staying awake for days
- Nervous eating or not eating at all
- Loss of interest in doing anything that always brought joy
- Feeling sad
- Weight loss or gain
- change in work habits
- Moving or talking more slowly or, being more restless or fidgety (so much so that others can notice)
- Ignoring phone calls
- Refusal to communicate with family or friends
- Making excuses for the sudden change in behavior
- Frequent headaches
- Developing a caviler attitude about your appearance i.e. hair, nails, and style of dress
- Negligent about your hygiene
- Defending a poor attitude

- Feeling like everyone is against you
- This fox makes you anxious
- He also makes his victims paranoid

This fox is shrewd, cunning, and extremely destructive.

The Fox of Low Self Esteem

Let's discuss Low self esteem. What does this fox do and how does he kill you.

If low self esteem is a fox that has entered your heart and taken residence in your home. He strips one of the ability to preform or function in almost every capacity of life.

This fox is a thief who robs every ounce of ambition, strength, and desire to move forward. In some cases, the low self esteem fox sends a whirlwind of insecurity causing the victim to feel in adequate with no hope of ever thinking he or she could ever achieve anything.

Here are some of the characteristics of this fox; he cripples and destroys your ambition, drains you of physical, emotional strength, and wherewithal to do anything. This fox feeds your brain with nothing but negativity not allowing any positive thoughts or ideas to flow. The fox blocks dreams and destroys any imagination or purpose for living.

The fox of Low self esteem gets into the emotions and thought pattern like a group of vines growing out of control until they choke the very life out of you if you let them. Negativity resinates within the victim 24 hours a day. The victims feel that there is no hope and that nothing positive will ever happen in his or her life. The fox of low self esteem backs his victims into a corner of doubt, mis trust, and disbelief in his or her self.

This fox causes confusion and violence in every home that he enters. Only Sarcasm and curt answers comes from the lips of his victim (s) with frowns that have made an imprint on their faces. They are always in a dark emotional place. His sly and cunning behavior transfers to all who come into his presence. He cunningly uses manipulation as a painter's color pallet to give illusions and a sense of false hope only to entrap those who stay in this vice. He moves and attacks when his victims are at their lowest mental state leaving them lifeless….His aim is to kill , steal, and destroy everything about his victims.

You have the option of letting him enter your home, heart and everything that you stand for and want to build or create or you can fight back.

Use the weapon of determination joy, happiness, love, and peace. Pull out the armory of determination, and positive thinking. Change locations of doubt, worry, anxiety and move to a place only propels you to the wonderful talented person that you are.

Toni never thought she could do or be anybody in life. She thought of an idea of opening up a business making unique jewelry, scarfs and pins. Toni was extremely talented However, every time she felt inspired, she was crushed with negativity that hit her as though a large sledge hammer was knocking her to the point of being unconscious. Her mother insisted that she could never be able to achieve anything like that; in fact, her mother thought of every negative thing she could to discourage Toni. Her excuse was that it wasn't going to work, where would she get the money to fund any of her projects or Ideas, and who would even purchase her product. Her mother picked apart every thing she ever made and went a step further by destroying some of the scarfs she designed by ripping them to shreds. Toni caught her throwing some of the jewelry in the trash and trying to destroy almost everything that she made.

Sadly, there was never a time that any positive encouragement ever came from her home.

The constant fighting and violence that took place was a trigger that sent Toni into a dark emotional place of low self esteem. She became confused with lots of brain fog and lethargy. All she did was sleep the entire day and night during her days off from working crippled by the fox that was in her house and heart. Work was sort of a place of escape because the work assignments had to have concentration and critical thinking. Aside from work, there were days that she could barely lift her head off the pillow after sleeping all night long. No matter how much sleep she received it did not take away the fact that she was always extremely tired and seemed never to get enough rest. Toni's facial expression painted a picture of how miserable and unhappy she was. The dark circles under her eyes deepened as she longed to be in a better emotional place. Curled up in a fetal position she longed for true love, a better atmosphere, and a chance to make, display, and sell her products. How could a change come about if this behavior continued she pondered day by day?

If this fox has entered your life, you will be the only one to make a change. Despite the effort, struggle, and the challenge, it is extremely important to engage in only positive things, severe all relationship ties that are negative, and run away from negative people that sabotage you as though your life depended on it.

Attach yourself to groups of people that are determined to make their goals become a reality. Avoid losers who talk but never move or make any attempt to change their way of living for the better. Associate with movers and shakers who make things happen. Make goal posters and tell yourself that you are an achiever and not a failure as your family or fair weather friends label you to be. Set time lines of start and completion dates and stick to each of them. Put energy, research, and time into preparing to leave your negative home or atmosphere. Let determination be your propelling force.

Toni gained miraculous emotional strength and started on a journey to fulfill her divine destiny. She was able to get an apartment not far from her job which cut down on the expenses that would have been used for transportation. The funds were redirected toward materials needed to make her products. A distance cousin who was moving out of the area gave her most of the furniture she needed which was another enormous savings.

One of her friends went grocery shopping and surprised her with enough food to last for a month. What a blessing all these things were and she was truly grateful. Her artistic ability was one to behold.

A number of Ideas that lay dormant for years was suddenly blooming like flowers at spring time. In fact, they were coming so fast that she could hardly keep up; just a short time ago the fox of depression had totally crippled her but now she was on a roll designing and making all sorts of things.

She signed up for a booth to sell her products twice month at a flea market which proved to be quite lucrative. A radiant smile now beamed across her face which changed her entire appearance. For once in her life Toni was interested in what she wore and how she looked. The frowns were gone, and her personality was totally changed. She was actually a very pretty woman but the depression had turned her into a totally different person. The co workers at her job could not believe the change or transformation that came over her. Whispers filled the office and the nosey co workers found the flea market where she displayed her products and made several purchases; They were shocked and amazed by what they saw and didn't waste any time to spread the news not only in the office but through out the company.

Her life had totally changed once she got rid of the fox of depression.

What ever you do, please don't let the Fox of Depression in your home or heart. If he happens to stop by, don't let him move in reside or linger throw him out immediately.

A Place in Your Heart for Seniors

Isn't it funny how for some reason seniors are pushed to the side, ignored and labeled as a burden once they reach the age that stops them from activities they did when they were younger.

The youth seem to forget all that the seniors did and provided for them not realizing that if they live long enough they will be old one day. Mother and Grand mother who once changed your diapers now needs a nurse to change hers. Her hearing is gone and she needs the assistance of a walker or a wheel chair to get around. That sharp memory is totally gone and there are times that she doesn't remember any of the family but constantly repeats every sentence of past experiences over and over again. Remembering only the things that happened years ago it seems that her short term memory seems to have short fused with no recollection of what is going on around her.

Many are bed ridden never able to walk or talk ever again. Body movements have turned into atrophy in both hands and feet for lack of use.

It wasn't that long ago that you could remember grandma jumping rope, playing basket ball, and running a marathon. There were even times that she could run up and down the steps without getting winded. It was though she never got tired.

But now, age, and sickness has gripped her poor fragile body, stripping it of all the functions that none of the family would have ever expected imagined. She no longer can swallow but is fed by means of a feeding tube full of liquids. A nurse has to bath and dress her making sure she is turned frequently to avoid bed sores that are painful and can reach her bones.

Growing old is bound to happen to everyone on planet earth so it is very important that while we are young that we take good care of our bodies by eating healthy and getting the right amount of exercised rest.

Take the time to visit, communicate, and be a help to grandma in what ever way that you can. Learn to put a smile on her face rather than a frown. Remember that she has more years behind her than in front of her.

Never forget the seniors. this will help them live longer and put lots of smiles on their faces. **Remember that you will become a senior one day if you live long enough.**

Don't Let any of the foxes enter your home or heart.

A Happy Place

The season of winter brings about a number of changes and adjustments through out the entire world. Homeless encampments are set up, make shift roofs over their life long belongings and their carts to weather the up coming storms, heavier clothing is required to keep warm, houses are warmed by fireplaces and furnaces. More fuel is required for various means of transportation, and the attitude of people seem gloomy and as sad as a dismal rainy day. As Winter roles back her curtain to make way for spring to make her entrance, the snow melts off the mountains, giving way to the beauty of the beautiful sky. The leaves change colors from brown and orange to a beautiful bright green.

But have you ever paid attention to how plants change their stature and flowers which were just seeds a few months prior begin to bloom in an array of colors and assortments that are simply breath taking. Birds change their living quarters and head for another habitat.

The ground becomes fertile and ready for planting. Seeds begin to bud growing in their initial stages waiting to be watered and nurtured by mother nature herself.

Hearts and emotions seem to fit into the mold as well. Attitudes seem much brighter because of brightness of the sunshine. Sunshine seems to bring laughter, lift up hung down heads, and put people in a happy mood. Clouds seem to take on a new form ; they give the illusion that anyone can just reach up to the sky and touch them. The sky color of powered blue gives a feeling that one could just rest in its presence and nestle there forever forgetting about all and everything and live as though one didn't have a care in the world.

Couples walk up and down promenades holding hands as they eat yogurt or ice cream sharing expressions of love.

High school seniors plan their career paths and begin to choose a college to attend that will help them achieve all their career goals.

Plans are put in place for engaged couples to choose a wedding date, pick venues for the ceremony, and choose the best rings that will last through out an eternity.

Schools prepare to shut down for the summer break and students look for a college or trade school to teach them a skill or prepare them for the career that will enhance their lives as they grow into adulthood.

New Curriculums are implemented for upcoming semesters as teachers meet with school boards to vote on what will be best for their schools in the fall of the year.

A lot of old things are thrown away to prepare for the new. Trash that took up space in our closets, corners, and even on our floors can all be thrown away. Spring and the sunshine that comes with it seem to do something in the atmosphere. Hung down heads are lifted, negative attitudes change to a more positive one, smiles increase, frowns disappear, moods brighten and changes take place all over the entire universe.

The most important thing about being in a an emotional happy place is that we can all change our emotional residence if need be . We can move and stay into a happy emotional place.

We can throw worry and everything the resembles damaging foxes are kicked out of our houses, minds, and most of all our relationships.

A Happy Emotional place becomes what we eat , live, and breath.

Every day that we live becomes a time in our lives that gives us an opportunity to make changes, implement new ideas and be determined to succeed.

You can Set goals and patterns in your life that limit the amount of stress that could cause you to have a stroke or a heart attack.

Please avoid the fox of Toxic fair weather friends that only mean to harm and not help you.

Stay away from foxes of fear, dysfunction, jealousy, envy, bitterness, and anger that could lead to destruction.

Prepare for the future with a sense of positivity believing in yourself that all your goals can be reached and that you will strive to make them happen despite any challenges and move full throttle to meet every time line set before you.

About The Author

Harriet Brooks is a mother and a grandmother of three children who live in Southern California. Through out her life she has worked tirelessly reaching out to the less fortunate in programs such as ADOPT A SCHOOL, ADOPT A BLOCK, FOOD GIVE AWYS, A GREETERS MINISTRY,
DRESS for SUCCESS seminars and many others.

Harriet Brooks is on a journey to walk in the destiny that she was designed before she was ever born. Despite a late start ; her passion is to reach all those who have been made to feel less than, battered, or discouraged to fulfill dreams or aspirations by people they have come in contact with who love to sabotage others.

Her desire is to encourage all who have been victimized and bring awareness letting them know that they are a part of a beautiful garden arrayed with gifts, talents, and abilities to walk in the destiny designed for them. What ever entrapment that you might have be come involved in, you don't have to stay in that situation . There is an escape route provided for you.

Please be aware of foxes of which a few were written in the book and refuse to let them in you house or heart.

Resources

1. National Suicide Prevention Life Line
Contact number 800- 273- -TALK 8255
2 The Sheep Fold Violence Shelter
Contact number 714 - 637- 1132

3.THE NATIONAL SUCIDE PREVENTION LIFELINE AT : 800-273-TALK 8255

4.**Mental Health America (MHA)** is the nation's leading community-based nonprofit dedicated to addressing the needs of those living with mental illness and promoting the overall mental health of all.

5. **The Depression and Bipolar Support Alliance (DBSA)** is a leading national peer-focused mental health organization, whose mission is to provide hope, help, support, and education for individuals who live with mood disorders.

6. United States Crisis Counselors 24/7
Contact number 800- 985- 5990

This information was taken from goggle.

I pray that what ever fox that might have entered you house or your heart has been completely destroyed or never entered because awareness.

Made in the USA
Columbia, SC
20 July 2022